High Brown Fritillary

Painted Lady

Small Tortoiseshell

Orange Tip

Small Copper

Small P...

Peacock

...bled White

Meadow Brown

Swallowtail

D0971300

CONTENTS

The Fireside Book

A picture and a poem
for every mood
chosen by

David Hope

Printed and published by
D.C. THOMSON & CO., LTD.,
185 Fleet Street, LONDON EC4A 2HS.
© D.C. Thomson & Co., Ltd., 1995.
ISBN 0-85116-607-5

SMALL AND GENTLE WAYS

TO sit before the hearth sometimes,
  And watch the flames leap higher,
Is not to see mere logs of wood,
Or just an open fire,
But, in the heart to know release
From all that tends to mar our peace.

To pick a bunch of daffodils,
In late or early Spring,
To roam and gather, where we will,
Is such a homely thing;
Yet, every single yellow bloom
Has power to set our minds in tune.

To walk in Autumn's rustling leaves,
As children do to town,
To count soft snowflakes, one by one,
As they come falling down —
These are small pleasures, that can bring
A wondrous sense of comforting.

To meet a friend, to read a book
To smile as smile we must —
These tiny things are things we do,
From morning until dusk;
As fragrant as a Summer breeze,
Are small and gentle things like these.

Margaret H. Dixon

CONTENTMENT

IN the early morning mist
we walk. Just the two of us.
One lost in thoughts.
The other in adoring.
You supply my needs and I yours.
And when we reach the open fields,
you leave me and run.
I walk, watching you, marvelling at your grace.
In the early morning mist
we walk. Just the two of us.
A woman and her dog.
Each content with her life
and wanting nothing save each other.

Marian Harper

HOPE SATISFIED

WHEN vixens scream like banshees in the night
 And brown owls wail their cry from leafless
 trees;
When hoar frost covers fallen leaves with white,
And pools that lie in hollows start to freeze,
I know the longest night and shortest day
Have come and Spring will soon be on its way.

When white-capped hills are streaked with
 brown and green,
And streams flow crystal clear from melting
 snow;
When pochards in display stretch necks and
 preen,
And geese in loose formation northward go,
Voicing in chorus their departing song,
Their music tells me Spring will not be long.

When wounded birch trees bleed and sap runs
 fast,
And creeping movement tops the wood ants'
 mound;
When brown protective sheaths from buds are
 cast,
And great tits claim their rights with bell-like
 sound.
I know the waiting has not been in vain,
And I have lived to see the Spring again.

John S. Groome.

THE POND

A RUSTIC village nestles by a spring
   Which feeds the pond of an abandoned mill.
At Summer noontide, laughing children ring
   About the banks; ducks splash to eat their fill
Of desiccated bread; dog owners fling,
   With cries of "Fetch", sticks on the water still.

I know that self-same pool at close of day,
   Devoid of people and their noisy cries.
The silhouetted alders fade to grey,
   A small bat skims the surface, hawking flies.
My line across the mirror snakes its way;
   I strain my vision, eager for a rise.

Brief hours of slumber later, back I wade;
   The light returns; a virgin day is born.
The pond, by steaming vapours overlaid,
   Is dappled by the golden shafts of morn.
By speckled trout, or empty creel, repaid,
   It matters not — I caught the dusk and dawn.

George Darwall

NIGHT PATROL

SOME nights, when cosy in my bed I lie,
   Upon my sleep-hazed ear there creeps a
   cry . . . "Daddy!"
My fumbling feet the slippers seek
And bear me to the children's room. I speak
In whispers and locate the wakeful bed.
"A drink of water!" says a tousled head;
Then, satisfied, returns at once to sleep.
But, ere I follow, first I bend and peep
At two such other forms of sleeping bliss,
And on their cherub cheeks impress a kiss.
Then back to bed, to lose the midnight chill
Within the welcome warmth of wool and twill.
Delicious languors soothe my broken sleep,
And soon upon the soporific deep I'm launched.
Thoughts ebb away in pillowed peace,
And memory and movements slowly cease . . .
But, hark! A call! Undoubtedly a daughter:
Another voice: "I want a drink of water!"

Noel Scott

SONNET FOR SPRING

HARSH Winter frosts and icy winds have bled
    The grass stones dry, and everywhere the cold
Brings all the trees into its silent fold,
The ballerina ash, with arms outspread,
The oak, rheumatic, with his stag-horn head
And knotted joints, it may be he's too old
Ever to reawake, can Winter hold
His life suspended? Is he alive or dead?

But light and warmth grow stronger day by day
To break the trance. The trees' slow blood is stirred
And pours through every vein, till on the hedge
Appears a dust of green, like down on bird,
And fast and feather-like the leaves will fledge
The boughs, and make a shining new display.

Katharine Macaulay

IN MY THOUGHTS

I COULDN'T see you today,
So I sent you my thoughts.
   Living and vibrant they sped through the air,
Out through the ether, through miles and through
      time.
   I hope you received them, and knew I was there.

I couldn't see you today,
So I sent you my love.
   It travelled through space like a bright, shooting
      star,
With the joy of the morning, the warmth of the sun,
   To wrap itself round you, wherever you are.

I couldn't see you today,
So I sent out a prayer,
   For I knew you were troubled, and heavy of
      heart.
And so with my thoughts, and my love and my
      prayers,
   Though distance divides us, we're never apart.

Iris Hesselden

THE OLD CORNISH RANGE

IT beckoned through a cottage pane
  With glowing coals and brass a'gleam,
My heart awakening at the sight
  Of childhood's long-forgotten dream.
And memories gathered round the range,
  Emerging golden on the sheath,
Tatie cake and saffron buns
  Beneath the Yuletide holly wreath.

I stood and gazed that Christmas night
  At iron cast with ornate skill:
High on the pine-wood mantel stood
  Two china dogs, a pipe and spill:
Upon the slab a kettle steamed;
  Cream gently rising off the boil.
Black-leaded iron and polished brass
  Shone with love and honest toil.

The wonders of the world I'd seen,
  And lands of wild silk, spice and tea;
Coral reefs and palm-fringed sands
  But none that brought such joy to me
As moon behind a tin-washed sky;
  Granite cliffs and wind-whipped foam:
A Cornish cove, a cottage small,
  That range the centre of a home.

Kathryn L. Garrod

SPRING MORNING

COMES the dawn, the winds of morning,
 Comes the light, another day.
Comes the sun, bright beams adorning,
 Brushing the clouds of night away.

Through the silence, early song birds
 Serenade the clearing sky,
And the seagulls swoop and hover
 To announce the tide is nigh.

Now across the gardens, creeping,
 Ginger tom cat, slinking home,
Weary from a night of hunting,
 Promises no more to roam.

Comes the dawn, with sounds of morning,
 Cheerful milkman on his way,
Bottles clatter and he whistles,
 Welcoming another day.

As the light is growing stronger,
 And the day goes on apace,
People wake and dream no longer,
 And rejoin the human race.

Comes the day that's now creating
 Light and life for everything.
Comes the time of celebrating,
 Comes the dawning of the Spring!

Iris Hesselden

WHEN I GROW UP

I'D like to be a man in blue
  Who walks his daily beat,
With shoulders squared and head erect
  And firmly tramping feet.

I'd like to be a general
  With troops at my command,
Or else a drummer playing in
  The regimental band.

Then I might be a sailor
  And cross the deep blue seas,
Or a lumberjack in foreign lands,
  Felling lofty trees.

I s'pose I could try carpentring —
  Carve fine things out of wood;
A chef in hotel kitchens making
  Lots of lovely food.

I could be a schoolteacher
  With blackboard, rule and chalk,
But all I do just now is dream —
  And wish for four o'clock!

Mary M. Milne

THE ROMAN WAY

THIS is the way the Romans came,
Advancing steadily over the hill,
This is the way they marched to fame —
And if you listen, you'll hear them still!
Men from Africa, men from Gaul,
Heading south from Hadrian's Wall,
For Rome, their mother, sent them all,
To carry out her will.

The road they trod reminds us yet
Of a mighty Empire that now lies still,
And we who follow won't forget
The Roman splendour, and the Roman skill;
And dreamers hear, when shadows fall,
The stirring sound of bugle-call.
Men from Africa, men from Gaul,
Marching over the hill!

Glynfab John

SPRING HOLIDAY

MAY'S the month of sun and showers,
  Skies of blue or clouds of grey;
Springing grass and nodding flowers,
  Streams that whisper, "Come away!"

May's the month when days grow longer,
  Fled old Winter's sullen chill.
Come away! The call seems stronger,
  From the distant, dreaming hill.

May's the month of blossom falling;
  Soon we'll take our holiday.
Heather-clad, the moors are calling;
  Birds are singing, "Come away!"

Peter Cliffe

SONG OF SILENCE

THERE is a silence in the woods,
   A silence comforting and deep,
When birds are mute, and every tree
   Stands motionless, in shadowed sleep.
When every little woodland flower
   Is under Summer's drowsy spell,
And many an ancient, mossy bough
   An old, bewitching tale could tell.
Then, in the calm and dreaming air,
   Along each dappled, ferny way,
The peace of centuries gone by
   Melts into stillness of today;
And in that hush, so absolute,
   There sometimes echoes, soft and clear,
A green wood song, which only those
   With ears, and hearts, attuned, may hear.

Kathleen O'Farrell

A DREAM OF GALLOWAY

I WILL return to the hills one day,
  To the land of the forests and fells,
To the Merrick and to Cairnsmore,
    To the Glenkens, Rhinns of Kells.
And I will tramp the hill tracks
    Where the tumbling burns flow,
To the haunts of the eagle and buzzard
    My spirit longs to go.

I will rejoice in the noonday sun,
    When the shimmering waters play,
And the glen reveals a blue lochan,
    A river of silvery grey.
While far away on the hillsides
    The red deer peacefully graze,
Where the grass is green in the corries,
    Nourished by long Summer days.

Then will I turn my steps homeward,
    To a house snug and warm at the sea,
By the ash, the oak and the birch woods
    'Neath crags of boulder and scree.
And there by the glow of the peat fire
    I will dream of the fells,
Of the Merrick and wild Cairnsmore,
    Of Glenkens, Rhinns of Kells.

Helen Bolton

THE SONG IN THE STREET

I HEARD a song at break of day —
  Some carefree traveller on his way,
Singing in the month of May,
Down in the street.

He sang of times he used to know,
In a world of long ago;
And one who set his heart aglow,
To make life sweet.

His voice rang like a golden bell:
How pure the notes that soared and fell!
As I lay caught within his spell,
Held by a dream.

At last his lovely song was gone;
His footsteps faded in the dawn;
And yet the magic lingered on,
In sunrise gleam.

Peter Cliffe

MAYTIME

O LOVELY, lovely Maytime,
    With cherry-blossom fair,
When cuckoo call is echoed
    Upon the scented air!
Come hear the blackbird sing so sweet
    Atop the hawthorn bough,
See flowers adorn the meadows, for
    'Tis almost Summer now.

O happy, happy Maytime,
    Fair stepping-stone to June —
Soft perfumed apple-blossom,
    The first sweet rose in bloom;
Come stroll with me by sparkling stream,
    And fill the golden hours;
Thank God for lovely Maytime gifts
    Of trees and birds and flowers.

Patricia McGavock

A MAY DAWN

NOW through the garden flows the dawn
  Like some full tide that bears
The coloured barque of day
Rich-laden on its breast.
Above the lawn a cypress lifts
Its sable sword in dark salute
To speed the waning moon and bid
Adieu to night.
The sun has yet to paint its shadow on the grass,
Still quilted grey with dew,
And no bird sings.
But on my senses steals a faint first scent
Of earth and newly opened leaves.
The breath of blossoms
Lingers as a lover's kiss,
Upon the lips of morning.
Wisteria climbs the eaves, and curled
Azaleas poise like yellow birds.
This magic hour in sleep to lose were vain,
And waking thus becomes my lasting gain.

Rose Ley

A FRAGRANT MEMORY

TODAY I stole two roses, I confess,
  Roses enhanced with crystal drops of dew,
Comparable to dawn's first loveliness,
  Revealing shades of ever-deepening hue.

The fragrant air stealing from the flowers,
  Evoked sweet memories of long ago,
When we shared together blissful hours,
  While love stole imperceptibly and slow.

Oh, that those times we undervalued then,
  Innocent, happy days so free from care,
Would come back, so that we might taste again
  The sweetness of the love we used to share.

Just as the petals flutter from the leaf,
Those hours now, it seems, were all too brief.

Phyllis Mary Mayfield

EVENING SONG

DEAR bird, who from the apple tree,
　　Sings songs so sweetly unto me,
Sing one more song to me I pray,
At this, the closing of the day.

Sing of March winds, that roar and blow,
After the cold of winter snow,
Preparing soon to welcome in
The gentler warmth of early Spring.

Sing of the clouds that ride so high,
In the clear blue of noon-day sky,
Sing of the softly falling rain,
When April showers return again.

Sing of the green of leafy trees,
In which you perch with careless ease,
Sing of the flowers of May and June,
Sing, little bird, a merry tune.

Sing from your gently throbbing heart,
Before the daylight turns to dark
A prayer to Him, whose constancy
Supports both you — a bird — and me.

Margaret Dixon

GARDEN MIRACLE

IT looked so bare in Winter's cold,
　What Springtime secrets would it hold?
But January brought buds of white
Close followed by bright aconite.

In February the crocus grew,
Then daffodils in March winds blew,
Tulips followed proud and tall,
Forsythia gold against the wall.

In June there opened fold on fold
Fair roses, pink and white and gold.
Why did I doubt in Winter bare,
That flowers would grow just everywhere?

Barbara Jemison

MIDSUMMER'S EVE

THERE'S magic alight in the heavens tonight,
  More magic than ever before;
The stars shine and glitter and hide in the clouds,
  And peep through the window and door.
The wind sings a love song to roses and thyme,
  While stealing their perfume away;
The warm earth is peaceful and holding her breath,
  And waiting for Midsummer Day.

Iris Hesselden

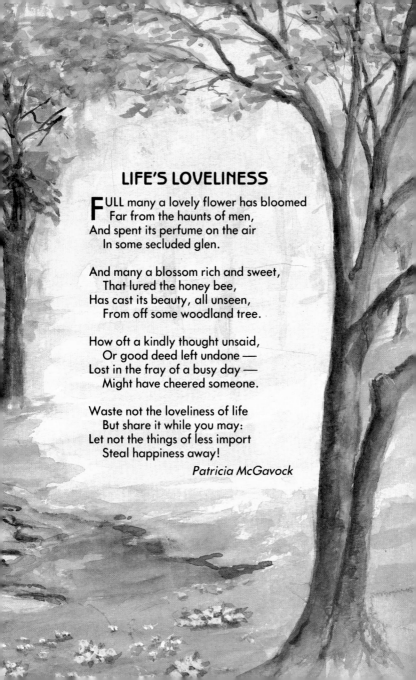

LIFE'S LOVELINESS

FULL many a lovely flower has bloomed
   Far from the haunts of men,
And spent its perfume on the air
   In some secluded glen.

And many a blossom rich and sweet,
   That lured the honey bee,
Has cast its beauty, all unseen,
   From off some woodland tree.

How oft a kindly thought unsaid,
   Or good deed left undone —
Lost in the fray of a busy day —
   Might have cheered someone.

Waste not the loveliness of life
   But share it while you may:
Let not the things of less import
   Steal happiness away!

Patricia McGavock

BOYHOOD

I LIVED in a valley, by green hills surrounded,
Through which flowed a river, long miles from
   the sea.
The vane on the church tower flashed gold in the
   sunlight,
   And rooks in the tall elms were ragged and free.

I fished in the river, caught newts in the duckpond;
  A tug on the line meant excitement and joy.
The meadows and byways in summer were my ways:
  I knew every spinney when I was a boy.

Then back with the sunset, the flittermice weaving;
  And glad to be homing, for I'd travelled far.
A light in our kitchen, where supper was waiting,
  That beckoned and guided me, just like a star.

Peter Cliffe

IN A FINE JULY

LOVELY day, you go too soon,
　Into limbo, and the high
Liquid splendour of the moon
　Quenches all the burning sky.

Yet in dusk about my feet
　Your elusive ghost reposes,
Breathing still of noonday heat —
　Grass and heliotrope and roses.

And long after you depart,
　Round the dim earth called away,
Waters of a quiet heart
　Mirror still my lovely day.

Audrey Field

SOLITAIRE

HE'S trod the dust of country roads,
  From Ditchingham to Dover:
Devil-may-care, from Heaven knows where,
  A brown-faced, laughing rover.

He bathes in rills at chill o' dawn,
  By wine-dark pools lies dreaming;
And takes his rest in a bracken nest
  When the Milky Way is gleaming.

He'll swing a scythe to earn his bread,
  Or pick sweet fruit in season;
Then off again, in sun or rain,
  And scorn to give a reason.

With ne'er a soul to call him kin,
  No friend or wife or lover,
He walks alone and cares for none,
  As wild as the moorland plover.

Peter Cliffe

INSOMNIA

NOTHING to fuss about,
   Nothing to keep me awake,
Nothing to worry me,
   No decisions to make.
No wind in the chimney,
   No lumps in my bed,
Just thoughts spinning round
   And around in my head.
The room is so silent,
   The night is so still,
I'll wait for the sun
   To peep over the sill.
I tried counting blessings,
   I tried counting sheep,
It's time to get up now,
   At last I can sleep!

Iris Hesselden.

MEMORIES

PLAY it again — once more that melody —
  That glad refrain; and as the charmed keys sing
Like rippling streams, our hearts will ring
With joyful echoes of another day.
Play your magic, moving symphony:
As birds rising to the heavens wide,
From olive twilights where they hide
Will flow the memories from the misty grey.

As haunted fragrance through a window blows,
Upon this Autumn day a breath of Spring,
Now Springtime heightens to the misted rose
Of bygone summers, and my feet take wing;
As lightly o'er the keys your fingers glance,
While you play . . . I will dance.

Eileen Melrose

ROSE IN BLOOM

PERHAPS it is a vain endeavour
　　To sing the praises of a rose;
No idle words of mine could ever
　　Portray the loveliness that flows
Through varnished leaves and stem, that bear
　　The satiny petals, curved to hold
Within a fragrant chalice there,
　　A store of honey-gold.
And so I think I'll be content
　　To say that, in this sombre room,
There glows — how heavenly the scent! —
　　A crimson rose in bloom.

Kathleen O'Farrell

BEAUTY

IT is Beauty itself I seek — not beautiful things!
    The something that shivers the heart when a
    linnet sings;
That colours the gossamer web on the whin at
    dawn,
And skies — that are not of this world — when day
    has gone.

The blue of the distant hills brings joy to me
As the scarlet rowan, the froth of the blackthorn
    tree;
Or the peace of the wine-red moor where the
    curlew cries,
And the love that shines through the soul in a little
    dog's eyes!

This is the Beauty I seek and desire to hold,
Woven into my being with skein of gold:
Ethereal: lifting me up above earthly things
Till I soar to the foot of God's throne — on
    Beauty's wings!

Sydney Bell

OLD SEA ROVER

O, I must away to dream now
　For the wind is o'er the sea,
And the mist has left the harbour-brow
Where the spume blows light and free.
O, I hear the sea-birds crying
O'er the bright waves' lush-green crest,
And they wake a wistful sighing
In an old sea rover's breast.

There's a twinkle in my blue eye
As the white sails hold my gaze,
There's the half-glad hush of a goodbye
To those weary long-shore days;
Then the old teak helm is creaking
As it slumbers in my hands,
And it seems to be a-speaking
Of those palm-fringed coral strands.

O, 'tis I who will rejoice then,
Sailing o'er those tropic seas,
Where a soul can be refreshed again
By the lotus-scented breeze;
As my ship heels sweetly over
In my fancy's pleasing flight,
The heart of an old sea rover
Dreams on in quiet delight.

Edward Borland Ramsay

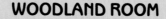

WOODLAND ROOM

THERE'S a winding path descending,
   Dusted gold with yellow broom,
Through a doorway of wild roses
   To a quiet, woodland room.

Its walls are leafy hawthorn,
   Faint-rustling o'er a ring
Of fairy carpet, violet-gay
   With bluebells in the Spring.

In Summer, mayflower curtains
   Drift to touch the floor,
Sun-stars at slatted windows,
   Bright broom garden at the door.

Rowan and elder tapestries
   Shimmer berry-bright,
A blackbird sings of joyfulness
   Somewhere out of sight.

But soon a frosted cobweb
   Will guard a leafless gloom,
My Winter heart will sigh and long
   For the rustling, sunlit room.

Eileen Melrose

THE NAMELESS BIRDS

THEY appeared, the wild birds, like a dream in
   the night,
Brown as the earth, but with under-wings white.
By a single desire they seemed to be moved,
As they rose in the air and circled and curved,
As if earth itself, in its need for the sky,
Took wing. Reedy and sweet came their cry,
Shaking the wind — and the tang of the sea
And the salt-weed smell of the estuary
Were suddenly here in this inland field.

Who are you, who are you, strange wild birds?
I want a name for beauty revealed,
I want to enshrine your beauty in words.
I have asked men wise in the wisest things.
I have searched great books to give you a name
(With the cry of the sea, and with moonlit wings)
But they will not tell, nor from whence you came.

Never since then have you wandered back;
But I know, oh, I know, Life's journey done,
When I count the goods in my traveller's pack,
The oft-sifted treasures, there will be one
Still wrapped in the joy of sudden surprise.
Those nameless birds will flash on my eyes
(Brown as the earth, but with under-wings white)
Who came once and passed, like a dream in
the night.

Lilian Maude Watt

I KNOW A GARDEN

I KNOW a garden
Where lilies grow
Full of grace and white as snow,
Where fragrant violets shyly hide
Neath love-in-a-mist
And London Pride.

I know a garden
With tiny pool,
Pink lotus deck the water cool:
Marsh marigold and sedge grow there,
Sweet evening stocks
Perfume the air.

I know a garden
Where songbirds trill
Midst thyme, rue, myrtle, lavender and dill:
Where roses sport soft shades of red
And scents and sounds
In peace are wed.

A garden where,
In passing by,
Under a blue and cloudless sky
Old Time slows down his hasting pace
A-while, capricious dreams
To chase.

Mary M. Milne

I WISH

I WISH that you were with me now
   To hear the thrushes in the beech,
The cuckoo hidden in the green,
   The heron on the muddy reach,
To see what countless Springs have seen —
   The lessons budding love can teach.

I wish that you were with me now
   To roam at will across the heath
Burned into gold by furze and broom,
   Until the stars their swords unsheathe,
And evening locks her secret room
   While clouds the bashful moon unwreathe.

I wish that you were with me now
   To glimpse the swallows dip and rise,
To hear the rooks in raucous choir,
   The murmur of the skimming flies,
The cows returning to the byre —
   The breathless tenor of my sighs.

In vain I wish you were with me
   To watch the swans' prophetic flight,
To listen to the nightingale,
   The river rippling with delight,
The brooding owl's nocturnal wail —
   I wish that you were here tonight!

Glynfab John

DAYDREAM

THERE'S an old road and a brown road,
   And a fingerpost leaning near,
Showing only nine miles to Barley Cross,
   So why do I linger here?

There's a small bird and a sweet bird,
   And it's carolling high o'er the hay,
While I'm dreaming of someone in Barley Cross,
   In the gold of a Summer's day.

There's a soft breeze and a warm breeze,
   And it's rippling a friendly stream
Which is wending its way to Barley Cross,
   With many a silver gleam.

There's a dear girl and a true girl,
   Who is all the wide world to me;
So it's time I set off for Barley Cross,
   With a step that is light and free.

Peter Cliffe

SEA SONG

THE sunlight sparkles on the sea,
  The wind is fresh, and wild and free,
And memories come crowding me
Along the old sea wall . . .

Those picnics shared upon the sands,
The busy, tiny, digging hands,
The dreams we dreamed, the schemes we planned
Along the old sea wall.

The old men smoked their pipes all day,
Remembered sailing far away,
So much to think, not much to say
Along the old sea wall.

But we were young and hurrying,
And life was swiftly scurrying,
No place for doubt or worrying
Along the old sea wall.

The cool, grey dusk is drawing near,
The memories are still warm and dear,
And I let fall a silent tear
Along the old sea wall.

Iris Hesselden

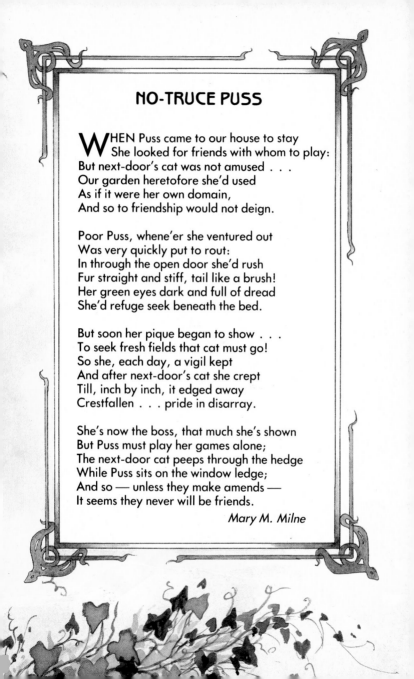

NO-TRUCE PUSS

WHEN Puss came to our house to stay
  She looked for friends with whom to play:
But next-door's cat was not amused . . .
Our garden heretofore she'd used
As if it were her own domain,
And so to friendship would not deign.

Poor Puss, whene'er she ventured out
Was very quickly put to rout:
In through the open door she'd rush
Fur straight and stiff, tail like a brush!
Her green eyes dark and full of dread
She'd refuge seek beneath the bed.

But soon her pique began to show . . .
To seek fresh fields that cat must go!
So she, each day, a vigil kept
And after next-door's cat she crept
Till, inch by inch, it edged away
Crestfallen . . . pride in disarray.

She's now the boss, that much she's shown
But Puss must play her games alone;
The next-door cat peeps through the hedge
While Puss sits on the window ledge;
And so — unless they make amends —
It seems they never will be friends.

Mary M. Milne

AUGUST

A TIME for the hay
And a time for the reaping,
A time for the fruit
For preserving and keeping.

A time to rejoice
For gifts in good measure,
For showers and rainbows
And moments to treasure.
For high, purple hills
And tall rushes growing,
For bright cottage gardens
And lazy streams flowing.

A time for the hay
And a time for thanksgiving,
For sunlight and laughter
And Summertime living.

Iris Hesselden

APPLES FOR REMEMBRANCE

A DEAR and lovely thing to see
Is this, the laden apple-tree.
I from her lowest branches take
Four apples for my childhood's sake.

One that I may remember still
The waving, yellow daffodil,
To lift me from the depths of gloom
When vanished is the apple-bloom;

One for high Summer, when in light
The tall elms quiver in my sight,
And when the small green apples hide
In leaves profuse on every side;

One for harvest and reapers brown,
When rough hands lay the sickle down,
And this tree drops her luscious fruit
In ripeness round the mossy root;

And one for when the driving rain
Sweeps o'er the upland and the plain,
When frost and ice chill to the bone,
And water freezes hard as stone;

And as these fruit I pick today,
I think of times long passed away;
Four reminders you give to me,
My dear and lovely apple-tree.

Glynfab John

A SONG TO MUSIC IN AUGUST

THE sun hangs high o'er Mary's spire,
  The air is sweet with Oxford chimes,
    And in my mind close-fitting rhymes
Play hide-and-seek until they tire,
While I go picking lavender, lavender,
Over the green lawns, under the apple-trees.

Along the valley, motors purr
    And like distasteful insects creep
    Over a coloured world, asleep
From One-tree hill to Shotover,
But I go picking lavender, lavender.

My lady in her hammock swings, —
    My lady is most beautiful —
    She binds the stalks with scarlet wool
And light of heart my lady sings,
While I go picking lavender, lavender.

Our minutes chime upon the breeze,
    The old tunes never sound again;
    But ever in my busy brain
I'll hear the mumbling honey-bees
And smell the swaying lavender, lavender,
Over the green lawns, under the apple-trees.

P. Hugh B. Lyon

INDIAN SUMMER

WITHIN the frosty glade
　　Across the rose hip spray,
Among the dappled shade
　　Summer lay;

In silence on the leaf,
　　In yellow on the grass,
Fragrance was the thief
　　Of Summer past.

And in the silent grove
　　Where chilly Autumn hung,
Imbued with Summer love,
　　Songbirds sung.

Eileen Melrose

EDGE OF AUTUMN

DRAINED is the Summer wine;
  Fallen, the rose.
Golden and bronze, the fine
  Chrysanthemum glows.

Restless, the swallow soars
  Over the trees;
Mist on the mounting moors,
  Chill in the breeze.

Painted, the woods. Too soon,
  Now, the day dies.
Orange, the harvest moon
  Burns in the skies.

Days of the best and worst —
  Summer's bloom lost,
Touched by the fragile first
  Finger of frost.

Brenda G. Macrow

AFTER THE HARVEST

TODAY it was Autumn on my mind.
  Out there,
On the plough and stubble,
Slanted rain.

A sharper edge I feel now
From the northern hills
To end the illusion,
Dampen the memories of richness gone.

The tints and flushes
Are drained from gold;
Reality dawns on a sodden mass of leaves
And barley grains lining muddied ruts,
Beneath long avenues
Of stripping trees turned brown.

In dripping emptiness
Fragile seed stalks stand out
Dark above the twisting grass,
Stand out meshed and strung
With wisps of woollen thread;
And spiders' webs hung torn,
Caught on the fleeces of mourning sheep
That wander by;

Still walking through the rain
Across the open, each alone.
Till even they are lost to sight
As mists are drawn across these festering skies . . .
The swirling wisps
Of a tattered gown outgrown.

Allan B. Brownlie.

GIVE ME AUTUMN!

GIVE me Autumn, gentle Autumn,
  When the torrid Summer yields
To the grey mist rising slowly
  O'er the twilight fields.

Give me Autumn, dreaming Autumn,
  When each golden apple glows,
And the dew clings like a lover
  To the last moss rose.

Give me Autumn, wistful Autumn,
　　When the brambles stain the mouth,
And the swallows come together
　　For the long flight south.

Give me Autumn, tranquil Autumn,
　　When the hollyhocks stand tall,
And the breeze begins to whisper
　　As the first leaves fall.

Give me Autumn, fleeting Autumn,
　　When the warning frosts begin,
And the cheery fireside beckons
　　As the nights draw in.

Peter Cliffe

I AM THERE

LOOK for me when the tide is high
 And the gulls are wheeling overhead.
When the Autumn wind sweeps the cloudy sky
 And one by one the leaves are shed.
Look for me when the trees are bare,
 And the stars are bright in the frosty sky,
When the morning mist hangs on the air,
 And shorter, darker days pass by.

I am there, where the river flows
 And salmon leap to a silver moon,
Where the insects hum and the tall grass grows,
 And sunlight warms the afternoon.
I am there in the busy street,
 I take your hand in the city square,
In the market place where the people meet,
 In your quiet room — I am there.

I am the love you cannot see,
And all I ask is — look for me.

Iris Hesselden

SAINT LUKE'S DAY

WHILE Summer died about my feet
   With frosty whispers in the breeze,
Love came, as crisp and late and sweet
  As apples in October trees.

Beside the still and shining fire
  I sat in peace, your presence giving
The fullness of my heart's desire,
  After the dearth of lonely living.

O last and best, go not away!
  But if you must, my dear delight,
The grace of this Autumnal day
  Will give me strength to meet the night.

Audrey Field

LIFE AND LOVE

"O LIFE is a thing," I pondered,
   "No man may taste in full,
From the patter of toes on the hearthstone
   To Age's brimming pool:
From youth's red dawn to the sunset
   Where the winds blow calm and cool."

You said — and the firelight glimmered
   On your hair and your darkling eyes:
"Dear! Love is the thing that matters —
   Leave worrying to the wise!
O Life is but whitening ashes
   When warm Love flickers and dies!"

Sydney Bell

MORNINGS

SLEEPY, cool September mornings,
  When the dew be-gems the grass;
And the stubble fields lie dreaming
  While the languid hours pass.

Shouting, shrill October mornings,
  When the wind's a merry thief,
Taking from the hapless hazel
  Fairy gold of every leaf.

Solemn, grey November mornings,
  While the pitter-patter rain
Dimples every tawny puddle
  Spreading in the old green lane.

Tranquil, blessed Christmas mornings,
  When there's ne'er a bird to sing;
But the peace of God lies over
  Snow-clad fields as church bells ring.

Peter Cliffe

WHO'S IN

"THE door is shut fast
   And everyone's out."
But people don't know
   What they're talking about!
Says the fly on the wall,
   And the flame on the coals
And the dog on his rug
   And the mice in their holes,
And the kitten curled up,
   And the spiders that spin —
"What, everyone out?
   Why, everyone's in!"

Elizabeth Fleming

WHY IS IT SO?

WHY do we fuss and fret and fume,
　　When there are trees?
Work ceaseless till late afternoon,
When there are bees,
Who, with such steady skill and pace,
Make honey, perfect to our taste?

Why do we lie awake at night,
When small stars peep,
Shining with gently twinkling light,
To guard our sleep?
Why toss so restless on our bed,
When all of Heaven is overhead?

Why think of just material wealth,
When there is sand,
The sea incoming — wave by wave —
To reach the land —
Treasure of grasses — blue of skies —
The wonder that around us lies?

Why do we fret, and fume and fuss,
When poppies grow
Scarlet in cornfields, near to us,
And west winds blow,
Breezes, that ruffle up my hair,
And prove that God is everywhere?

Margaret H. Dixon

The artists are:—

Charles Bannerman; When I Grow Up, Song Of Silence, Apples For Remembrance.

Sheila Carmichael; A May Dawn, Life's Loveliness, I Wish, Indian Summer, Edge of Autumn, I Am There.

John Dugan; Sonnet For Spring, The Roman Way, The Song In The Street, Old Sea Rover, I Know A Garden.

Allan Haldane; Hope Satisfied, Midsummer's Eve, August, After The Harvest, Mornings.

Harry McGregor; The Old Cornish Range, Spring Holiday, Insomnia, Memories, Sea Song, A Song To Music In August.

John Mackay; The Pond, Boyhood, Rose In Bloom, Daydream.

Norma Maclean; Evening Song, Beauty, Give Me Autumn, Life And Love.

Sandy Milligan; Spring Morning, A Dream Of Galloway, In A Fine July, Why Is It So?

Douglas Phillips; Small And Gentle Ways, Contentment, Night Patrol, Garden Miracle, Solitaire.

William Young; Woodland Room.

Staff Artists; In My Thoughts, Maytime, A Fragrant Memory, The Nameless Birds, No-Truce Puss, Saint Luke's Day, Who's In.

Purple Emperor

Clouded Yellow

Comma

Common Blue

Brimstone

Silver-Spotted Skipper

Wall

Small Heath

Red Admiral

Scotch Argus